JEWISH
FESTIVALS AND TRADITIONS

by Emily Raij

PEBBLE
a capstone imprint

Published by Pebble, an imprint of Capstone
1710 Roe Crest Drive, North Mankato, Minnesota 56003
capstonepub.com

Copyright © 2025 by Capstone. All rights reserved. No part of this publication may be reproduced in whole or in part, or stored in a retrieval system, or transmitted in any form or by any means, electronic, mechanical, photocopying, recording, or otherwise, without written permission of the publisher.

Library of Congress Cataloging-in-Publication Data is available on the Library of Congress website.
ISBN: 9780756594336 (hardcover)
ISBN: 9780756594381 (paperback)
ISBN: 9780756594374 (ebook PDF)

Summary: Readers curious about world religions can explore the meaning and customs behind major Jewish holidays and festivals, including Rosh Hashanah, Yom Kippur, Hanukkah, Passover, and more important Jewish days.

Editorial Credits
Designer: Dina Her; Media Researcher: Jo Miller; Production Specialist: Tori Abraham

Image Credits
Getty Images: Godong, 5, Sam Feinsilver, 17, Scott Harrison, 8; Shutterstock: Attitude, background (throughout), blueeyes, 21, Brandon Koykka, 27, ChameleonsEye, 25, Donna Ellen Coleman, 23, Drazen Zigic, 1, 11, 12, FamVeld, cover (top), Katy Lozano, 28, Magic cinema, 15, Nelson Antoine, 29, Nodar Chernishev, 14, Pixel-Shot, 7, ungvar, cover (bottom); Superstock: Glasshouse Images, 18

Any additional websites and resources referenced in this book are not maintained, authorized, or sponsored by Capstone. All product and company names are trademarks™ or registered® trademarks of their respective holders.

Printed and bound in China. 6098

TABLE OF CONTENTS

Introduction to Judaism 4

Rosh Hashanah and
Yom Kippur...6

Hanukkah 10

Passover 16

Life Events... 22

Glossary 30

Read More 31

Internet Sites..................................... 31

Index.. 32

About the Author 32

Words in **bold** are in the glossary.

INTRODUCTION TO JUDAISM

Judaism is a religion celebrated all over the world. Jewish people believe in one God. They have their own culture, **customs**, and holidays. Many Jews say **prayers** in the **Hebrew** language.

Jewish people believe in living a life of holiness. They follow the laws of the **Torah**. They do good deeds called mitzvot. Some Jews eat only **kosher** food. Many Jews place a mezuzah outside their front door. This is a small case with a prayer scroll inside. It reminds them that home is a **holy** place.

The Torah scroll contains the first five books of the Hebrew Bible.

ROSH HASHANAH AND YOM KIPPUR

Jewish holidays follow a **lunar** calendar. Dates of holidays change each year with the phases of the moon. Every holiday starts at sundown but may last from one to eight days. Holidays end at night when there are three stars in the sky.

Rosh Hashanah is the Jewish New Year. It happens in the fall. People use this time to think about their actions over the past year. They also celebrate the creation of the world.

One **tradition** is eating apples dipped in honey. This is a symbol of the new year's sweetness. Another tradition is to blow a ram's horn, or shofar. It is a wake-up call to remember God.

Apples dipped in honey are eaten during Rosh Hashanah to symbolize a sweet new year.

Synagogues are at the center of many Jewish communities.

Yom Kippur is 10 days after Rosh Hashanah. Jews ask for forgiveness from God and those they may have hurt with their words or actions. Many pray in **synagogue**. Some do not eat or drink for the whole day. This helps them think about how to act better. Afterward, they enjoy a festive meal.

Rosh Hashanah and Yom Kippur are part of the High Holy Days. They are the holiest days of the year. A traditional greeting during these holidays is "Shanah tovah." That means "good year."

HANUKKAH

Hanukkah is an eight-day festival. It celebrates religious freedom for the Jewish people. Many years ago in Jerusalem, a Greek king would not let the Jews practice their religion. His army ruined the Jewish temple.

A small group of Jewish soldiers fought back. They rebuilt their temple. They had to look in the old temple for oil to light their menorah, or lamp.

In the Hebrew language, the word *menorah* means "lamp."

The helper candle sits in the middle of the menorah. It is called the shamash.

According to tradition, there was only enough oil to light the menorah for one night. Somehow, the menorah stayed lit for eight nights.

Today, a hanukkiah, or Hanukkah menorah, holds eight candles. A helper candle lights the others. Each candle represents one day. Every night, a new candle is lit. By the last night, all eight candles, plus the helper candle, are glowing. This is why Hanukkah is called the Festival of Lights.

Other Hanukkah traditions include singing songs and giving small gifts. Children play a dreidel game. A dreidel is a small spinning top with four sides. Letters of the Hebrew alphabet decorate each side.

Sufganiyot have been the official food of Hannukah since the 1920s.

Eating foods fried in oil honors the Hanukkah story. Favorite treats are jelly doughnuts called sufganiyot. Another is potato pancakes, or latkes. They are topped with applesauce or sour cream.

PASSOVER

Passover is a spring holiday. It is also called Pesach. Passover lasts eight days. It celebrates freedom. Long ago, the Jews were enslaved in Egypt. They escaped in the middle of the night and carried what they could.

The people did not have time to let their dough rise. It baked flat in the sun. The flat bread is called matzah. During Passover, people give up risen, or leavened, bread and eat matzah instead.

Families sing, pray, and tell the story of Passover during their special holiday meal.

The Haggadah contains the story of Passover, prayers, blessings, and songs.

Other special Passover foods help Jews think about what it was like to be enslaved in Egypt. On the first and second night of Passover, families gather for a special meal called a seder. Seder means "order."

During the seder, Jews read the Haggadah. This book tells the story of escaping slavery. Many people sing songs or pray. The Haggadah explains the order of the meal and when to eat different foods from a seder plate. The plate has spots for each food.

There are five Passover foods on the seder plate.

- Charoset is a sweet mix of fruit, nuts, and honey, juice, or wine. It is meant to look like the clay enslaved people used to build things in ancient Egypt.

- Bitter herbs such as horseradish remind people of the bitterness of slavery.

- Parsley or another green vegetable is a reminder of spring. It is dipped in salt water, a symbol for the tears of the enslaved.

- A roasted lamb bone is not eaten. It represents sacrifice.

- A hard-boiled egg also symbolizes sacrifice and the circle of life.

Passover foods

LIFE EVENTS

Jewish parents are responsible for their children's actions. When a Jewish child reaches the age of 13, it is time for a ceremony called a bar or bat mitzvah. Boys have a bar mitzvah. Girls have a bat mitzvah.

During this time, the child becomes responsible for completing God's commandments. They read from the Torah at the synagogue and talk about what they learned from the reading. It takes years to prepare. There is often a party or meal afterward to celebrate the hard work.

Commandments, or mitzvot, encourage good deeds and actions.

23

Jewish couples are married under a canopy called a chuppah. At the end of the ceremony, the groom steps on a glass. Guests shout "mazel tov!" That means "good fortune."

When a Jewish person dies, family members make a small tear in their clothing to show their sadness. After the funeral, there is a period called shiva. Family and friends comfort the mourners at home.

Loved ones are remembered. People light a special candle and say a prayer on the anniversary of their death.

The chuppah symbolizes the home the bride and groom will make together.

Shabbat is the Jewish **Sabbath**. It is a day of rest each week. Shabbat starts Friday at sundown.

Jewish people honor the Sabbath in many ways. Many Jews light Shabbat candles. They say blessings for wine and a braided bread called challah. Some Jewish people will not work, use electricity, or drive on Shabbat. Many Jewish people pray at synagogue.

Challah

While at synagogue, Jews wear a head covering. It is called a kippah. They also wear a prayer shawl called a tallit. Shabbat ends Saturday at sundown with a special ceremony called Havdalah. A braided candle is lit. A blessing is said over a cup of wine and sweet-smelling spices.

Jewish people are proud of their faith. They honor their beliefs all year long.

A kippah is also called a yarmulke.

GLOSSARY

custom (KUHS-tuhm)—a tradition in a culture or society

Hebrew (HEE-broo)—a language used by ancient Israelites and modern-day Jewish people

holy (HO-lee)—dedicated to God or a religious purpose

Judaism (JOO-dee-iz-uhm)—a religion and culture based on a belief in one God and the teachings of a holy book called the Torah

kosher (KOH-shur)—prepared according to Jewish dietary laws

lunar (LOO-nuhr)—having to do with the moon

prayer (PRAY-uhr)—a request or an expression of thanks to God

Sabbath (SAB-uth)—the Jewish day of rest, from sunset Friday to sunset Saturday

synagogue (SIN-a-gog)—a building where Jewish people come together to pray

Torah (TOR-ah)—the law of God in Judaism; the first five books of the Hebrew Bible make up the Torah

tradition (truh-DISH-uhn)—a custom, idea, or belief passed down through time

READ MORE

Hagander, Sonja, Matthew Maruggi, and Megan Borgert-Spaniol. *Religion around the World: A Curious Kid's Guide to the World's Great Faiths*. Minneapolis: Beaming Books, 2022.

Singer, Marilyn. *Awe-some Days: Poems about the Jewish Holidays*. New York: Dial Books for Young Readers, 2022.

Wills, Anna. *Who Believes What?: Exploring the World's Major Religions*. Berkeley, CA: Owlkids Books, Inc., 2018.

INTERNET SITES

BBC: Key Facts About Judaism
bbc.co.uk/bitesize/articles/zfn792p

Kiddle: Judaism Facts for Kids
kids.kiddle.co/Judaism

PJ Library: Jewish Holidays
pjlibrary.org/holidays

INDEX

bar mitzvahs, 22
bat mitzvahs, 22

candles, 12, 13, 24, 26, 28
clothing, 24, 28

dreidel game, 14

foods, 4, 7, 15, 16, 19, 20, 21, 26

Hanukkah, 10, 13, 14, 15

marriages, 24, 25
menorahs, 10, 11, 12, 13
mezuzah, 4
mitzvot, 4, 23

Passover, 16, 17, 18, 19, 20, 21

prayer, 4, 9, 17, 18, 19, 24, 26

Rosh Hashanah, 6, 7, 9

Shabbat, 26, 28
synagogues, 8, 9, 26, 28

Torah, 4, 5, 22

Yom Kippur, 6, 9

ABOUT THE AUTHOR

Emily Raij has written more than 40 books for children and edited dozens of professional resources for K-12 teachers. She is a native of Chicago, where she earned her journalism degree from Northwestern University. She lives in Florida with her husband, daughter, son, and dog.